Making Cartonera Books

Making Cartonera Books
Experiences in Cardboard Book Publishing

Daniele Carneiro and Juliano Rocha

Translated by Adrian Minckley

Library Juice Press
Sacramento, CA

Published in 2025 by Litwin Books.

Litwin Books
PO Box 188784
Sacramento, CA 95818

http://litwinbooks.com/

This book is printed on acid-free paper.

The brand names of products and stores, and the names of institutions contained herein are intended to demonstrate the cartonero book making process. The names are not advertisements, nor are they endorsements.

Names: Carneiro, Daniele, author. | Rocha, Juliano, author. | Minckley, Adrian, translator.
Title: Making cartonera books : experiences in cardboard book publishing / Daniele Carneiro and Juliano
Rocha ; translated by Adrian Minckley.
Other titles: Sobre livros cartoneros: experiências em publicação de livros de papelão. English.
Description: Sacramento, CA : Library Juice Press, 2025. | Summary: A personal account of the authors'
experiences with their handcrafted, in-home, and independent publishing house, started in 2014.
Identifiers: LCCN 2025938841 | ISBN 9781634001816 (paperback)
Subjects: LCSH: Magnolia Cartonera. | Cartonera books. | Cartonera books – Publishing – Latin America. |
Cartonera books – Publishing – Social aspects. | Self-publishing.
Classification: LCC 231.5.L5 C37 2025 | DDC 070.509--dc23
LC record available at https://lccn.loc.gov/2025938841

Contents

Hello and Welcome

This book is a personal account of our experiences with Magnolia Cartonera, our handcrafted, in-home, and independent publishing house. Since 2014, we've been writing, publishing, and crafting cartonero books, which are books with handcrafted carboard covers, as well as zines, which are small self-published magazines made entirely by hand and independently.

When we say handcrafted, we mean that our books are made from cardboard boxes we collected ourselves. We repurpose, paint, sew, and bind the cardboard by hand, and the only machine used during the entire process is a home printer. That means we work with paint, thread and needles, cutting tools, scissors, and our home printer. It also means that the production process relies entirely on manual labor, so that every time we create a new copy, a new story begins.

Aside from sharing our experiences, our goal is to offer practical information and helpful ideas to strengthen your desire to publish cartonero books with covers made by hand. We want to encourage and support people who are thinking of going into independent self-publishing, but who haven't found the literature to help them understand the process of handcrafting a cartonera.

We understand that part of our work as independent artists is to share information about our own practices of writing, publication, and graphic arts at Magnolia Cartonera so more people are able to access it. This book is our attempt to help anyone who wants to establish themself as an artist or writer create their own cartonera books and publishing houses.

Although lots of people know about cartonero books in our communities, we've noticed that the simple techniques of hand binding carboard boxes to make them into book covers remain largely unknown.

Through this text, we hope you learn Magnolia Cartonera's techniques for manufacturing books and that you feel encouraged to write and to publish. We wrote this book for people who want to cultivate and strenghten their own autonomy over their creative efforts.

We'll show you how we got our start and how we carry out our daily cartonera activities to inspire you to do the same.

We'll describe the initial stages of creation, from assembly to the finishing touches, all the way to advertising and selling our books. We'll talk about the most important, interesting, and motivating details anyone looking to dedicate themselves to cartonera art will need. You'll read about the reasons why we want more people to be able to work creatively and make a living through the art of writing, publishing, and manufacturing books with cardboard covers.

This book is personal because it's our story. These are experiences we have lived as part of Magnolia Cartonera within the world of DIY publishing and the ways we found our path to cartonera art, now laid out on the page.

Making cartoneras requires a lot of work, energy, time, ability to overcome adversities, some financial investment, and, more than anything, the desire to make it all happen.

Ever since we first started, we've invested everything we have—our labor, available resources, energies, and art—into the activities of planning, writing, illustrating, editing, publishing, crafting, and selling cartoneras. It has been an incredible journey.

In this book you will find a combination of ideas, inspiration, knowledge, tips, and insights from people who are already making it happen. We hope you find the inspiration and support you need within these pages to forge your own path.

Daniele and Juliano
August 2019

A Walk Through Our History

We had been involved with free, community libraries and projects incentivizing reading for a few years when we created the blog *Bibliotecas do Brasil* (Libraries of Brazil blog) in 2012. Ever since, we've been publishing texts, articles, and ideas about book sharing, as well as acting as a database for all kinds of libraries, with a principal focus on autonomous projects that promote the circulation of books among readers.

In 2014, we started publishing *Newsletter Expresso*, a periodic, informative, and free email we send to readers discussing interesting topics from the world of books, libraries, art, cinema, science, art, and technology.

As we gained more experience with independent projects, we felt it was time to share our art beyond the virtual world and publish our ideas on paper. To do so, we had to take a big leap forward.

Because of our increasing need to publish our work, we started developing a book project, and we knew immediately it would have to be a DIY publication. It wasn't realistic for us to chase after traditional publishers nor could we afford to bankroll the cost of publishing a book through a printer. Our budget was close to zero, so those options just weren't available to us. During the first few months of 2014, we reflected deeply on what resources we could put toward making publishing a book a reality.

When we found cartonera books, it was a transformative moment. We got in contact with handcrafted publishers for the first time at FestiPoa Literária, Porto Alegre's literature festival, where we participated in the release of an art book by Jornal Boca de Rua at the Encontro de Saraus de Porto Alegre, on the 25th of May 2014, at the Casa de Cultura Mário Quintana. The book, *Boca de Rua*, was a cartonera that brought together stories, poetry, and crônicas—a Brazilian genre of short-form writing—stapled into issues of their newspaper of the same name, which is created and sold by the city's houseless community under the coordination of the Agência Livre para Informação, Cidadania e Educação (ALICE – Free Agency for Information, Citizenship, and Education). The cartoneras, crafted with cardboard covers sewn by hand, were decorated by visual artists who were supporters of the project.

We immediately understood that this was the perfect way for us to start publishing and disseminating our books. We didn't want nor did we know how to get in touch with publishers, and we didn't want to subject our creativity to anyone's authority. We wanted total autonomy over the editorial process: to write at our own rhythm, choose fonts, do the editing, and above all, create our own visual identity. And in the process, learn to make a book.

We went back to Porto Alegre excited to make a cartonera book, and over a three-month period we collected our texts and organized the materials we had at home that could help us craft the book itself.

We printed 15 copies at a printer who charged BRL $.08 (eight centavos) per printing, we collected the cardboard boxes from multiple locations, we painted and crafted the covers, and we released it on the internet. Since we didn't know anyone doing cartonera workshops, we studied how to sew them by watching crafting and sewing tutorials on YouTube. It was through watching these textile artists share their knowledge online that we started to decode, learn, and utilize the manual skills needed to make cartoneras.

With cartonero books, we were able to fuse our artistic interests, talents, and abilities together, and in August 2014 our first publication was released, called *Cartonera Bibliotecas do Brasil (Libraries of Brazil Cartonera Book)*.

Simplicity

Making Cartonero Books is dedicated to people of all backgrounds and life experiences. We're using the same simple, light, and accessible language here that we use in our Magnolia Cartonera books and zines and on the Bibliotecas do Brasil blog. We're intentionally sharing our ideas and lived experiences in easy-to-understand writing so that the largest number of people possible can understand our message.

Feel free to skip information you already know how to navigate with ease but always maintain empathy for and solidarity with people who will be walking this path for the first time.

We raise awareness about and collect information useful to people who don't have easy access to resources and tools for crafting and publishing books, who live in remote areas, who don't have a computer or easy access to the internet, and who encounter barriers to finding stores and markets that sell crafting materials in their cities.

We offer a warm welcome to people for whom cartonero books are something new, a path full of discoveries to behold, challenges to overcome, and who are excited to get to work. We also started from zero with almost no money to invest in handcrafted books, and the text you hold in your hands is the result of years of struggle.

We'll be having this conversation in simple terms, with an open heart, and we hope to find your spirit in that same state, too.

Part 1
Information

Cartonera Practices

Making cartoneras is a popular cultural practice within the world of DIY publishing. It is a manifestation of graphic, visual, and handcrafted arts and a literary movement that began in Argentina in 2003 which today enjoys a large presence in other Latin American countries, as well as in North America and Europe. There are people dedicating themselves to cartoneras in all corners of the globe, people using art, digital media, and creative writing to bring their work to life.

The cartonera practice involves handcrafted book binding using repurposed cardboard covers, as well as the self-publication of limited editions, allowing people to produce their own books at more accessible prices, both for those publishing the books and those buying them.

During the height of the Argentinian economic crisis, when funds for production and printing were scarce, independent artists started creating handcrafted books on their own. They printed them at small print shops or on home printers and reused cardboard to make the covers, painting and sewing each one by hand, making each cover unique. Cartonero publishing is an opportunity for people to forge an alternative path toward publication that is untethered to conventional publishing houses.

The word *cartonera* comes from the word *cartón*, which means cardboard in Spanish. *Cartoneras* and *cartoneros* are people who collect recyclable material, principally cardboard, on the streets of Buenos Aires and sell it for money.

The relationships between cartonera publishers and people who collect recyclable materials are varied and can take the form of cardboard collectors publishing their own books or cartonera authors and publishers buying the cardboard that will later become book covers directly from collectors.

Just as the internet gives a voice to all voices, cartonero books give a voice to all people, be they writers, poets, artists, educators, recycling workers, or anonymous individuals who use these publications as a way for their work to become known and read.

Handcrafting books, even when done by collectives, is not a process of mass production. You can complete the entire process of writing the book, creating a visual identity, illustrating, publishing, and printing all by yourself. To make it possible, interested parties need to want to make the books and utilize the tools, materials, and abilities they have within reach. The books are then exchanged between artists and the reading community without an intermediary and can gain the support of universities, libraries, cultural centers, educational professionals, bookstores, fairs, and independent literary events. Making cartonero books is a beautiful, diverse, manifold, open, and free activity for all people.

At Magnolia Cartonera, years of experience have shown us that making books with cardboard covers is a practice where people who are disadvantaged, who don't have access to the resources to publish conventional books, and who have been systematically excluded from the world of art and literature can finally have access to the means to create.

People without formal education can shine at cartonera art because this practice doesn't limit itself to academic accolades, isn't restricted to the world of diplomas, masters, doctors, or the gatekeepers of art. Students can come into contact with a form of popular art that isn't available within the world of institutional academia, a practical art that is learned informally and which originated from the people.

Although rules and customs can emerge through daily practice, they only apply to those who create them and hold no sway over any other practitioners of the art. Each of us works according to our own conscience and in the ways we deem correct.

Any cartonera artist or publisher who wants to exist and express themself, exists and expresses themself. Each cartonera artist or publisher has their own fundamental principles for how their work should be carried out. Do what you want, as long as it doesn't infringe on or exploit another.

This is why the cartonera practice is revolutionary, because anyone can access it. The possibilities for expressing artistic talent and creativity aren't centralized within an elite, making it possible for artists from the periphery and those who are underprivileged or low income to engage with the public directly.

People interested in cartonera art can work individually or in a collective. They can collect cardboard on their own from markets and commercial establishments. They can buy the cardboard directly from collectors and recycling cooperatives. Collecting cardboard on your own or working directly with recycling collectors is a question of editorial preference and of what is best and most viable for your personal cartonera art practice. The fact that the book has a cardboard cover doesn't disqualify the work and doesn't diminish it's "literary value."

The cartonera practice doesn't subscribe to any one value system, nor is it subject to outdated conventional market practices or literary canons. Cartonero books exist on their own merit; they are sold, traded, shared, studied, sent to other countries, and the only ones deciding their relevance are their readers.

During the research for this book, we discovered that the diversity of the cartonera experience even extends to the spelling of the word "cartonera." In Brazil, we found spellings that added an "i," like, "cartoneira" and "cartoneiro," as is more typical of the Portuguese language than the Spanish "cartonero." We've also found that, even though the word for cardboard in Portuguese is "papelão," over the years that we've been saying and writing "cartonero" and "cartonera," people have understood that we're talking about our books with cardboard covers, about our publishing house, Magnolia Cartonera, and referring to ourselves as cartonero and cartonera writers.

People are free to relate in whatever way they see fit to the books, to the editorial process, to the writing process, to the pronunciation, and to the practice of cartonera. You decide the best way to define your work, your art, and your practices.

Cartonero Books

Cartonero books value the autonomy and freedom of artists on the margins producing work based in their realities, ideologies, writing styles, and the places where they live, which are generally outside of already established and consolidated literary scenes.

This publishing style is a powerful tool for amplifying authors that lack support or visibility, who want to publish their literature independently and on their own timeline. Because cartonero books can be published using whatever materials a person has on hand, they offer the freedom to choose any theme, genre, or language that can be printed, painted, glued, and sewn between two pieces of cardboard. Anyone can publish a cartonero book even if they lack technological resources using whatever size budget is financially viable for them.

The practice of making cartonero books is not only an assertion of independence, it's an act of resistance that offers artists the chance to follow an alternative path, even in the face of trying times, like the Argentinian economic crisis.

The practice of making cartonero books brings people into contact with their inner artist, since making a book requires making hundreds of creative choices, from what font will be used to what color string will bind the cardboard cover to the pages.

The autonomy this practice provides is enormous and allows for the addition of small details that make your books unique. The freedom of not having a defined path can be scary at first, but with each step you take you'll realize that the pleasure of holding your ideas in your hands, in the form of a book you made yourself, is one of the best things ever.

Thanks to the rise of the internet and digital interactions, nowadays very little of our artistic production is tangible, and sometimes our work and creations never take shape beyond our computer or phone screen. You could even make a connection between cartonero books and 3D printers, since both give form to ideas that were previously only digital.

Literature and art are machines that generate empathy; by diving into another person's reality, you lose your fear. In that moment, the pain and pleasure of others become our pains and pleasures. Different voices are necessary to create new narratives about what it is to be human and to amplify understanding between diverse groups of people.

Handcrafted

Handcrafted art is enormously important today because it embraces human potential, amplifies people's autonomy, and gives individuals who have been systemically excluded from the art and publishing worlds a voice they wouldn't otherwise have.

Cartonero books are not mass produced or standardized, churned out in large quantities on an assembly line using automated processes that deliver complete and finalized products, like, for example, the pieces that make up a car. They also can't be compared to conventional books that are published by editors in industrial printing warehouses using mass production techniques in which millions of copies are produced in the blink of an eye.

The creation of this book you are reading right now required human hands and eyes attuned to countless details—not to mention time and dedication—before it was ready. The process of crafting each of Magnolia Cartonera's books involved artistic labor done by hand. Naturally, it takes more time to complete a book that way, because there's a person spending the time to bind it. Even though our handcrafted productions vary in their quantity, details, and the time it takes to finish one, the books are all made one by one with the same level of care and integrity.

Our cartoneras are made with the help of various tools, all handheld, like a box cutter for cutting cardboard, an awl for piercing the paper, and sewing needles and thread for binding. The only machine involved in the production is a home printer for printing the book's content, which is the pages containing the text.

During manufacturing, numerous kinds of cardboard boxes are used and, when made into book covers, react in different ways to being painted, folded, and sewn. That's how the handcrafted practice of cartonera makes each book unique.

The Cardboard Is the Star

Cardboard is everywhere in our society, and it accompanies us in many of our daily activities. Used to transport and protect products in the form of packaging such as boxes for food, clothes and shoes, store windowpanes, stands, and machinery, it has infinite uses, and we often don't even notice it's there.

This resistant material can be found in complex configurations with multiple thick layers or in the form of a single, light adornment. When we go out collecting, we find all kinds of boxes. They can be corrugated or not, smooth and blank or covered in logos and product and factory branding.

Cardboard is a strong, abundant raw material, with 260 billion square meters produced annually the world over to carry every type of object from books, electronics, and furniture, to the food and clothes we use every day.

Even though most people don't recognize its relevance or value, cardboard is extremely useful to humanity and is the main source of income for families all over Brazil, as well as other Latin American countries, thanks to money earned from collecting and recycling it.

Through conscious hands and creative minds, a material often thrown away as "trash" is now being transformed into the most varied works of literature, art, poetry, activism, education, politics, and all kinds of manifestos that have a lot to teach us about a culture of sustainability.

Over the past few years, we've noticed an uptick in interest in recycling and how to use cardboard for artistic expression like painting, sculpture, literary arts, as well as for recreational uses of the material as a toy.

Maker culture is pushing us to rethink the way we consume products, how we recycle, reuse, and transform materials into new objects, and how we can create all kinds of things using only our hands.

Cardboard now has a place in classrooms, libraries, contemporary art galleries, and museums, because creative people are making objects through recycling and discovering new possibilities for reuse. Now, a material that would have been thrown in the trash can be art.

In order to craft a cartonero book, we collect cardboard boxes that have already been used to ship products and are available in grocery stores for people to carry their purchases home in. The boxes vary in brand, size, color and texture. We always select boxes in the best condition: those with firm cardboard that is clean, free of tears and staples, and without crumples.

After collection, the boxes are cleaned so they can move on to be cut, painted, have the printed pages sewn to them, then be pressed, packaged, and shipped.

It's important to keep in mind that this is a process of reusing a cardboard box that was made for other uses, like the protection and transport of products. Even after being cleaned, painted, and sewn—once the books are ready—they may still give off the smell of cardboard or paint.

These books look rustic and natural, they might have some rough spots they obtained during cutting or folding or contain imperfections inherent to the cardboard itself, but this doesn't lessen their value or quality.

We take care of all the finishing touches, we make any cosmetic improvements needed and leave the logos of brands and products the box already had on the inside of the covers, and apply a light layer of paint when we deem it necessary. That way, the Magnolia Cartonera books keep their soul as cardboard boxes.

The boxes are our manifesto, and our aim is to show that cardboard boxes can be transformed into beautiful book covers without having their memory erased. We want readers to have that feeling of surprise when they look at the inside covers and see the brand there, the product type, the sticker with the lot number, the bar code, or the name of the market where we collected the boxes. That way they know that the cardboard kept its identity even after we transformed it into a book cover.

This is the most illustrative form of showing that a box made for holding and transporting goods can have a second and completely new existence when reused. By leaving the information exposed on the inside of the cover, the cardboard boxes continue to tell their story even as they take on new meaning. Every person who dedicates themselves to making cartonero books will make their own editorial choices about how to paint the covers and handle those details for themselves.

Artistic Expression

A cartonero book can be a way to showcase your artistic abilities, be they writing, photography, illustration, digital arts, painting, or sewing. Making cartoneras is a process of constant learning and you might even awaken talents you didn't know you had. With cartoneras, you can try out all kinds of art, get involved in multiple projects at the same time, and who knows, maybe start dedicating yourself full-time to making books and earning an income from them.

Art never stops changing and the biggest difference in the cartonero format is that it gives you freedom of creation. Your voice, your mark, and the pixels that come straight from your soul find endless possibilities in the form of pages to be filled. By learning the basic techniques of the art of cartonera, the power to publish books blossoms in front of you, and the end result is beautiful and unique.

This is an opportunity for you to come connect with your curious mind, that thing that since childhood has craved to know how things work on the inside. After a few attempts, or often just one attempt, you'll be holding the book that used to only exist in your mind in your hands. There's lots of space to grow within the field of DIY publishing, and it's waiting to be populated with new ideas like yours. Alternative books and artists are here to fill the gaps the editorial market has yet to discover and to meet the people's demand for content that has yet to be addressed and developed. Those are the ideas we need, even though they're missing from our bookshelves, bookstores, and libraries.

Labor and Time

Projects that involve art and literature require periods of dedication. Prepare yourself to dedicate creative and productive hours to your art, writing, and the development of the skills that will be your tools during your cartonera process.

Making handcrafted books takes all kinds of creative labor, from thinking about how the book will look to writing it, not to mention the illustration, editing, printing, and crafting.

You also need to consider how your books will be promoted and how they'll make it into people's hands once they're ready. All of this work is work, and you are the person responsible for creating your own schedule. Throw yourself into your craft and make the clock work for you. By making conscious choices about your time, you'll soon have an idea of what works for you and what doesn't.

Dedication

To transform your book into reality will take 100% of your will-power, the efforts of your labor, and your intention to make it real. Remember that only you, your collective, or group of supporters can make this idea into reality. We all start somewhere, and no one is born knowing everything. Believe in yourself as someone capable of learning to build, sew, knit, fix, mend, paint, or whatever other activity the moment requires. If you don't know how to do any of those things, use this book to start learning how. As you'll see in these pages, you'll need to complete a series of hands-on tasks before your book is finished, but if you take it one activity at a time, before you know it, you'll be done.

You should know now that if you don't already know how to sew or use a box cutter, you'll need to watch some videos on our YouTube channel (you can find the address in our link section). That's how we got started, watching the work of people who have been dedicating themselves to crafting since long before we ever started. Sewing a cardboard book and cutting cardboard aren't complicated activities, but if you've never sewn before or you feel you've never had the chance to develop your crafting skills, seek support and use the resources available to you to learn how.

Since the support we offer consists of this book and the resources we've made available on the internet—via the Magnolia Cartonera and *blog Bibliotecas do Brasil* websites and our YouTube channel—keep in mind that in order to make a cartonera the way we do, you'll need to learn how to thread a sewing needle and how to sew the book pages to the cardboard cover. We'll walk you through every step in the crafting process in as much detail as possible, but only you will be able to decide if the binding of the cover is tight, if the cardboard you collected is ideal, if the cover was cut correctly, or if you need to switch the blade of your box cutter.

We want you to be confident in your work. Just like us, you're learning. You are responsible for your cartonero project and for your journey as an artisan. Read and reread the chapters and, when you need to, try again with what you've learned from this book. Rely on your good judgement and your idea of what's right to make sure your books are following the path you desire.

Creating the Book

This is the initial phase, even before thinking about crafting the covers. It's the time when you should let your ideas guide you and just write. Think about the reason the book exists, the story, the content, the genre, the words, the message, the illustrations, and the art you want to put out into the world. Think about what utility the book will have to readers and define the age range of your reading public.

Write → Arrange chapters in an order that makes sense → Make corrections and edit the excess → Develop the book's visual identity → Think about the details → Publish.

Cartoneras With or Without Computers

For people without access to a computer who would like to use one to write and edit their books, there are libraries, reading centers, and community computer centers that offer computer services. Seek these out in your city or via LAN cafes. Talk to professors and people who work in education who can help you find a computer to use. Your local government likely also offers information about spaces that promote digital inclusion. Smartphones and tablets have text editing software and if you have those tools, it would be a great idea to learn to use them.

You won't need a computer if your cartonera book will be in a more challenging format, one entirely based on writings, clippings, collage, drawings, and art created by hand. You also have the option to use a typewriter if you have access to one, the same way zines are often made today. Draft a document that will act as a template for your book, and then all you have to do is photocopy it.

Part 2
Materials

When we started thinking practically about how our cartoneras would be crafted, the first thing we did was collect all the materials we had at our disposal. Because it was impossible at the time to invest in purchasing anything, we focused on what we had at home. Working with the resources available to us is the principal motivation for our endeavors, be it cartonero books or creating free, community libraries. We encourage others to do the same. Focus your thoughts on the abundance you have in your life.

The quantity of objects we have at home, and which are often lying around without being used, can be surprising. You can give new, functional life to stagnating objects through the manufacturing of cartoneras. Then, we started getting organized and thinking about what each step of the creation process would look like, which was entirely new to us. We learned how everything happens by working with the books. Now, we share each of those steps with you.

Start With What You Have Now

Gather the Materials

Start at home. Gather everything you have that is in good condition and can be used in cartonera activities. Search in drawers, boxes, dressers, and collect everything you find like needles, scissors, paint, pencils, pens, felt-tip pens, markers, packing tape, masking tape, rulers, printer paper, cardboard boxes, and fabric. That's how we started Magnolia Cartonera, we opened drawers and boxes and surveyed what we had in terms of paper, school supplies, and arts and crafting materials.

Donations

Relying on the support of people you know and trust is an interesting place to start your work with handcrafted books. Talk to people in your circles who can help you by donating materials and tools. Tell people what materials and tools you need and use social media to spread the news about your donation drive. You can also send emails or speak personally with people who may be able to assist you in your creative efforts.

Make Lists

Making a list of things you need to do is an excellent way to keep everything organized. It can be in a notebook, a notepad, on your phone, or on a computer. Work with what's easy. The list will help orient you so you can remember what materials you already have, what you need to buy, and the things you need to get done. Organization helps prevent surprises, especially if you start working with delivery deadlines. By making a list of materials you already have, you can anticipate what you'll need in future productions. If the stores where you need to buy materials are located far away, always keep an eye on what's in stock, even if you work with small amounts of materials, to avoid surprises.

Space to Work

Your workspace can be your kitchen or living room table, a desk, a bench, a garage, or somewhere in your yard. Taking apart cardboard boxes, cutting them into covers, cleaning and then painting them requires a lot of work. Then, they'll need to stay in a ventilated area that is protected from water and dust so the paint can dry. Afterwards, the covers will go through a process of sewing and binding on top of something that can support your tools and your book, like a table. Once the books are completed, they'll be packaged and ready to be sold and sent off to readers. Think of what space is available to you where you will have the freedom to make a mess and then organize it later without having to worry.

Budget

After gathering your materials, you can establish a small budget to buy whatever you may still be missing and to make eventual replacements. Within our cartonera practice, the acrylic paints we use to paint the cardboard covers, the printer ink, and the printer paper are the materials we use with the highest price and turnover, which is why we always have to buy more of them. But some tools, like the box cutter, the awl, and the cutting mat, we only bought once. The materials end up being paid for by the money generated by book sales, which you can reinvest to create a stock of supplies you need for production. If used wisely, these tools can last years in your hands. The printer ink as well as packing materials, like glue, tape, bubble wrap, and envelopes, are things we always have to replace due to the quantity of books we produce and send out.

Selling Cartonero Books

There's an important question regarding writing and publishing handcrafted books that you have to ask yourself from the beginning: Will you sell your cartonero books? Reflect on whether or not you're interested in earning your own income from them. The world of DIY publishing is just that: done yourself. As creators, we have to exercise autonomy over our creative labor.

If we need to support ourselves with our creations, be it in order to cover personal expenses or to maintain the self-sufficiency of our cartonera process, we're free to choose to monetize the work.

But know that the moment you start working, you'll start getting requests for free books, "comped" books, or offers to trade. Giving away books for free is a personal editorial decision, and it's also a chance to put your autonomy into practice, especially if you need to generate income from book sales. You'll need money from sales to maintain the flow of materials, to finance upcoming projects, and to cover other expenses. It's up to you to decide when to say yes or no to giving your cartonera books away for free and to define the limits of what's acceptable. Always keep in mind what is most viable for your handcrafting process.

Money

One common misconception is that making cartonero books doesn't cost any money, despite the fact that we live in a world where everything costs something and everything has a price. Yes, it is possible to create without utilizing money by using recyclable, self-sustaining materials that are easy to access in some cities, like, for example, collecting cardboard for free at supermarkets. But if you need transportation to collect it, whether that transportation be your own or a private or public service, or if you need to buy the cardboard from collectors and recycling collectives, those are transactions that involve money.

You can save a lot of money by collecting donations of materials from supporters, but the other activities involved in making cartonera books will always require some amount of money in some way. A few examples: if you are printing the cartonera books at home, you'll need a budget for the printer ink, the quantity of which will vary depending on the demand there is for your books. If you do the printing at a printing press or copy store, you'll need to pay for the quantity you order. Paints for painting the covers also cost money. When you send the books through the mail or via private courier, you'll need to spend money on packaging, envelopes, and shipping costs, the same as you'll need to buy and maintain some amount of materials during production.

Make yourself aware of the fact that yes, there is money involved and invested from the beginning to the end of the process of making cartonero books. But if you adapt your workflow to your budget in practical and economical ways, the process becomes completely sustainable via book sales. Produce the books according to your needs and based on the budget you have available to you. At Magnolia Cartonera, we don't buy all the materials we use all at once. We spend small amounts throughout the year, as necessity demands or as we're able to afford them.

Our idea since the beginning has been to maintain book production active throughout the entire year, and to do so, we need the money created by sales. If you prefer, choose to do small, limited runs for a defined period of time and set budgets for each. You can do seasonal productions and cater your publications to a public you're able to serve with ease. Taking breaks between publications and defining the budget needed for each period is also an option you can choose to take.

Materials for Each Step of the Crafting Process

1. Cutting the Cardboard

<u>Cutting mat</u>

The cutting mat is a resistant and durable mat that provides a base for cutting paper, fabric, plastic, and other materials. It's sold in a variety of sizes, colors, and brands. We use a 60x40cm mat for cutting and sewing the cardboard covers. You can substitute a wooden, glass, metal, or MDF base instead. Sheets of glass or metal that are the same size as the cover can be used as a mold for cutting. If you're using a glass base, be extra careful with the box cutter, because it slips more easily on smooth surfaces.

Box cutter

The box cutter is one of the main tools in cartonera art. It's worthwhile to invest a little more of your budget on professional box cutters and a blade kit, because they're more durable and precise, which is important in this work. The blades are retractable, and as soon as they get dull the tips can be snapped off with pliers or using the slit in the handle of the box cutter itself so the tool can continue to be used. The box cutter blades are divided into small segments and have lines where they can be snapped to reveal a new tip. A sharp box cutter blade will save you a lot of time and effort in your cartonera art.

Ruler

We use metal rulers to mark where the cardboard will be cut. They work better with the box cutter blades, allow for more precise work, and don't leave frayed edges after cutting. Wooden and plastic rulers can also be used. By working with the cartoneras, you'll discover the materials that are most practical and accessible for you.

Pencil

This is used to draw the measurements on the cardboard for where you will cut and later to mark the places on the book pages where the holes will be punched.

Rag or piece of fabric

The cardboard releases chunks and pilling during the crafting process. The rag is used to remove that excess and keep your work area clean. During sewing, the thread also tends to shed. A rag or paper towels are also used to clean the covers with rubbing alcohol.

2. Sewing and Assembly

<u>Sewing cord</u>

Sewing the covers sustains the binding and makes the book more durable. We use synthetic embroidery thread, which has a great finished look. It's a thicker and stronger type of thread that keeps the books bound tight and looks great. You can use string or yarn. You can find a variety of sewing products and different kinds of cord in different thicknesses, textures, and colors. Choose thread and string that you find practical and that won't deteriorate easily.

<u>Needles</u>

We use embroidery and tapestry needles to sew our cartoneras because they're thick, resistant, and have a nice finish. We're sharing the information from the packaging of the needles we usually buy so you can look for it at your nearest store if needed: "Hand sewing needle for embroidery, 20 count, size 2." They're really durable. Small sewing kits with multiple needles can be found for sale in most places and always have one more solid needle used for thicker string, which can also be used for sewing cartoneras.

<u>Awl</u>

An awl is a pointed tool that punches the holes in the paper where the needle and thread will pass through when the book is sewn. Consisting of a thick, rounded wooden handle and a metal shaft, this tool is known as an awl and makes a huge difference in a cartonera practice. The awl is used to pierce the cardboard covers as well as the book's contents, or the pages containing the text.

The tool with a slightly longer handle and same metal shaft can be found under the name "stitching awl." There is also something called a "fine tip awl," which is smaller and lighter weight.

3. Painting

Paints

We use acrylic paint for artists found in jars or tubes to paint the cardboard covers. We really like acrylic paint because it dilutes well in water, comes in bright colors, and when it dries it forms a protective film on the cardboard that protects against moisture. It makes for really nice-looking work and has a nice finish. Fabric paint didn't seem as efficient as acrylic, because it requires a lot of time to dry and ends up feeling sticky on the cardboard. But these are our personal experiences, feel free to test whatever kind of paint you want.

There is a huge variety of paint in the art world to experiment with. We've used gouache paint during a workshop before because it was what the participants had available at the time. Gouache paint is one of the cheapest paints for sale and is better suited to small budgets, but it tends to crack, lessening the work's durability. Another option is to use permanent markers, which you can find in a huge variety of colors, or pens that use India ink, also known as technical pens, to fill in details and create more elaborate designs. Technical pens tend to be more expensive than markers. An even cheaper alternative is to buy India ink in 20mL jars and apply it directly to the covers using the dropper that comes with the ink or with a brush, depending on the desired effect.

Brushes and objects for painting

You can use any object you want, like brushes, marbles, stamps, spatulas, yarn, and pretty much anything else to paint your covers. We use our own hands in the majority of our paintings. This is the time to let your imagination guide you and express your creativity. Having a few absorbent rags, a roll of paper towels, and a bowl of water helps a lot when painting.

Drying the covers

We use a section of our living room next to a window to let the cardboard covers dry and air out. We cover the floor with large pieces of cardboard, newspaper, or with an EVA mat. During painting, the paints give off a strong smell, but after the covers dry the smell goes away. Don't put the covers out to dry under direct sunlight or the heat will deform the paint and make the colors dull. To guarantee they are completely dry, we leave the covers out for 24 hours. Notice how long it takes to dry, because this will vary depending on the humidity in your area. A tip for making the process faster is to put a fan in the area where the covers are drying.

4. Printing

Paper

We use 75g A4 white sulfite paper (similar to US letter size paper), used widely for printing and writing, and because it's more common, it can be found at all kinds of places, like grocery stores, stationary stores, and office supply stores. Use whatever type of paper you like; you can even change the color of the pages within a book by using colored paper.

Printers

Your book can be printed on any home printer—inkjet or laser—that takes size A4 210x297mm paper or similar. Depending on what goals you want to achieve with your cartonera publisher and the size of your budget, you may consider buying a printer so you can have more control over your work. Printers that can automatically print on both sides of the paper save time because the pages don't need to be reloaded manually. Printers with an ink tank as opposed to ink cartridges make printing a lot easier. We use an Epson EcoTank L4160, but for two years we used a cheaper model that doesn't automatically print on both sides, the Epson EcoTank L120.

When we first started our cartonera practice, and during the two and a half years that followed, we printed our books at various copy shops until it became unsustainable to continue. We had a hard time finding copiers near us that offered quality, affordability, and good service, not to mention one that would reprint copies that got streaked by the toner in their machines. Buying a printer was an investment to improve the quality of our books. It made the work cheaper and allowed all steps of production to be done at home. The investment was well worth it for the autonomy it gave us over our own work and the fact that it ended the problems we were having with copiers.

5. Packaging and Shipping

If you plan to sell your book once its bound, you'll need to package it so you can ship it. From the simplest packaging to the most elaborate, you'll find a vast world of colors, formats, materials, possibilities, and prices. If it's within your budget, choose eco-packaging, which generates less impact on the environment or packaging that can be recycled after use.

The packaging needs to be practical for the person receiving the book. We take care to wrap our cartoneras in bubble wrap before putting them in the kraft paper envelope to protect them during shipping. We do it that way because the materials are within our budget, they're resistant, and they protect the books from harm. Search in packaging and crafting stores, at stationary stores, and in grocery stores to find your ideal packaging.

Search #dicasmagnoliacartonera (#magnoliacartoneratips) on Instagram to see pictures of our materials.

Where to Buy the Materials

Access to stores specialized in arts and crafts varies a lot from one city to the next. Make a list of the stores near you and keep an eye on sales and promotional offers. Here are the places where we find materials:

Haberdasheries, stores that sell small items for sewing and crafting

For buying needles, sewing thread, scissors, paint, rulers, and box cutters. In crafting stores, we buy the cutting mat and the paint at a more affordable price than in stores that specialize in art and drawing supplies.

Packaging supply stores

For buying envelopes, bubble wrap, and kraft paper for larger orders. These stores tend to have hidden products, like really good scissors and box cutters at better prices than at stationary stores and craft stores. Keep an eye on areas that are tucked away to find what you need hiding at great prices.

Homewares stores

.99 stores sell a little bit of everything and are a great resource for buying materials and finding useful tools for your cartonera practice.

Grocery stores

We collect cardboard boxes for our covers and usually find deals on A4 paper for printing our books at our local grocery store.

Stationary, school supplies, and computer stores

They're great options for buying basic materials like printer paper, box cutters, pens, pencils, pencil sharpeners, erasers, and envelopes.

Art supply stores

Stores that specialize in art and drawing supplies are more expensive, but they have a wider variety of products, as well as imported goods. You can find almost everything you need there. Always have your list with you so you can check if any of the items you need are on sale.

Scrapbooking and quilt stores

For buying the cutting mat, needles, sewing thread, awls, and other materials. We always visit them to see what's new with these stores in our area, but their prices are hardly budget friendly. Keep an eye out for one in your neighborhood and visit it to check pricing.

Online stores

The internet is full of online stores where you can find the materials you need to make your books with the ease of home delivery, generally plus the cost of delivery. Lots of physical stores also have online stores, so choose your favorites and always make sure they're credible before buying.

Part 3
Crafting the Book

Collecting the Cardboard

Cardboard boxes can be collected in all kinds of markets, stores, buildings, and residential buildings. Cardboard can be bought from recycling cooperatives, warehouses, and associations. It can also be bought directly from recycling collectors. By buying from recycling collectors, your publishing project strengthens their profession. In the book *Ideias para Bibliotecas Livres* [Ideas for Free Libraries] (Magnolia Cartonera, 2015), we dedicate an entire chapter to discussing how we can directly contribute to professional recycling collectors by collaboration between cooperatives and libraries. We urge you to get to know more about that work.

If your neighborhood isn't near any grocery stores, talk to local business owners about collecting cardboard boxes, like clothing or shoe stores, corner stores, local markets, produce stands, pharmacies, and furniture and homewares stores. All these choices are valid, and it is entirely up to you or your group to decide how you go about your work. This is your editorial decision, which will be made per the terms you agree to along with the person you decide to buy your cardboard from. Choose what's most practical, sustainable, and more importantly, viable for your cartonera process and which won't be exploitative of cardboard recyclers.

Choosing Boxes and Sanitization

As soon as you start collecting boxes and transforming them into book covers, you'll understand the dynamics of cardboard and how the material behaves. Some boxes are made of more fragile cardboard that falls apart when cut. Others are really durable, made with a type of cardboard that has double or triple layers, but they're hard to fold. There's thick cardboard, thin cardboard, firm cardboard, and cardboard that's too fragile to hold the pages. Cardboard is never the same from one box to the next. Through the practice of collecting and cutting, you'll figure out what boxes are best for the work you want to do. We prefer malleable yet durable boxes that are easy to fold and which only contain one layer.

We only choose clean boxes that don't smell like the products they carried, and which aren't smashed or torn. Because cardboard boxes have an internal ribbed layer, you can see lines on the outside of the box. To make the covers, we leave the lines in a vertical position, since the cardboard folds and settles better that way, and there's less risk of the cardboard breaking when handled. This gives the cartoneras a nice finish and makes them malleable when leafed through.

Cutting

Magnolia Cartonera's books have the following measurements: lying flat, the cover forms a rectangle that is 34 centimeters long by 24 centimeters tall. We use the cutting mat on a table, a pencil, and a 50cm ruler to mark the measurements on the cardboard boxes, and the box cutter and large scissors to clean up the edges.

Start by taking apart the cardboard box, cutting off the inner and outer flaps. Cut all sides of the box by following the folds until you can spread open the box into one solid piece.

Then, all you have to do is cut each side of the box to separate it. Take care not to crush the larger sections, as those will be transformed into covers. Depending on the size of the box, all four sides can be remade into covers. Now, use the cutting mat on top of a table to support each of the cardboard pieces while you transform them into covers. Use your pencil to mark the measurements of the rectangle (34cm x 24cm) on the cardboard, and using the ruler to guide the box cutter, cut out the cover using straight lines.

Once it's ready, remove excess and clean up areas that were cut unevenly using the scissors. Measure the cover and check that the dimensions are correct. If the cover is misshapen, use the ruler and the box cutter again to even out the sides. Sanitize the covers with a rag lightly moistened with rubbing alcohol and let it dry. Don't use too much sanitizer or you might damage the cardboard or give it too strong a smell. Now the covers are ready to be painted.

Painting and Drying the Covers

When using paint to make the cardboard cover art, make sure to cover the table and work area with newspaper, kraft paper, or whatever protective material you have on hand. This offers protection against paint splatter and drips.

Painting the cover is an expression of your creativity, so use whatever technique makes you happiest (painting, collage, drawing, sewing) and let your hands go wild.

Folding the Covers

Each box is different. Do tests and observe the cardboard's malleability, how it folds, and how it settles. Once the cardboard is cut into the shape of the book cover, fold it slowly from the center. Because it's a thick material, some covers will put up resistance to being folded. The cardboard doesn't fold like a piece of paper, so you need to use your hands and fingers to get the crease of the cover's center just right. The base of the awl can be helpful here. When folding the content pages, separate them into groups so you don't hurt your fingers and so they align with each other and the cover better.

Printing

Printing the books can be done with inkjet or laser printers, depending on your preference and what you have access to. It can also be done at a print shop, at a photocopy shop, or at a LAN café. If you make your cartonero books using collage or a typewriter, you only need to make one template and then as many copies as you want. Look for printing and photocopying services in your city at stationary stores, markets, LAN cafes, and copy shops.

Punching holes in the covers and pages

Secure the pages to the cover. Place the cardboard cover you have already painted and folded with the inside facing up in a horizontal position on top of a flat surface, like your cutting mat. Position the printed pages which you have already folded on top of the cardboard cover. Visually confirm that the pages are well-aligned with the cover's edges. Between the pages and the edge of the cardboard, there should be around 1.5cm (one and a half centimeters) of space.

Use metal binder clips or large clothespins to secure the pages. This ensures that they stay aligned and don't move when marked with the pencil, which guarantees precise puncturing. Clothespins are cheaper than binder clips, but for books with a larger number of pages, binder clips are more effective.

Holes. When binding the book, decide how many holes the inside pages will have. The holes will allow the needle and thread to pass through the pages so they can affix the paper to the cardboard cover. The more holes, the more times you'll have to pass the thread through. At Magnolia Cartonera, we use three holes.

We use a pencil and a ruler to mark where the holes will go on the pages and an awl to create them. The first hole is made 7 cm (seven centimeters) from the top edge of the page. The second hole is made at 10.5 cm (ten and a half centimeters) and the last hole is made at 14 centimeters. As soon as the holes have been punched, the book is ready to be sewn and bound. *Take a look at the online, downloadable, and printable poster for more details.*

Sewing

Once you get to the sewing phase, celebrate! Your book is on the final step before completion! The sewing we do at Magnolia Cartonera is simple and efficient at keeping the pages and the covers together and the binding tight. For someone who has never held a needle, sewing can be a challenge. You'll need your willpower and ability to learn, because this is another essential phase in making your book a reality.

To learn how to use a needle and thread, do some sewing tests on pieces of fabric or pieces of paper you've folded in half. We also recommend this approach for people who have some familiarity with sewing but who haven't done it in a long time.

This part of the crafting process isn't complicated and the more you use your tools the better you'll understand how they work. Get to know your work materials and remember that you're not competing with anyone. We learn how to improve by trying. Now is the time to learn and make your cartonera art into reality.

Learn how to put the thread in the needle. In order to make it easy to put the thread through the needle, use scissors to cut off the tip of the thread so it's nice and clean. Once you've threaded the needle, there's no need to make a knot. That will happen at the end, when you wrap up the sewing phase.

Sew. The sewing we do is very simple. It consists of passing the thread through the holes in the book up and down successively, until the cover and the pages are secured tightly to each other. We start at the middle hole. Check the drawings on the poster that accompanies this book to learn the sewing steps. Put the thread through the needle, hold the end of the thread opposite from the needle down onto the book itself using your thumb, and pass the needle and thread through the pages using the middle hole, with the needle pointing down. The needle will come out on the side with the cardboard cover. Turn the needle so it's facing up and pass it through the top hole, passing through the book from the cover side, back to the side with the pages. Now, pass the needle through the middle hole again and go toward the bottom hole. Pass through the holes up and down until you've filled them all with at least three layers of thread. Finally, leave some extra thread at the end so you can make a knot once you've ended on the pages side of the book. Then tie a few more knots so your thread holds firm.

Pressing

Pressing the books is the part of the finishing process that helps the pages of the cartonera book stay aligned with the cardboard. Because the cardboard is a resistant material, this process ensures that the covers lay flat, flush, and in harmony with the pages.

To press, we place our already bound cartonera books on top of the cutting mat then place a stack of heavy books on top. Use whatever flat, heavy object you have available on a flat surface. We use printer paper or kraft paper to protect the painted covers from direct contact with the cutting mat and with the heavy books we place on top.

Numbering and Signing

Limited edition books can be numbered or signed by their authors to distinguish each piece in a set. For example, a book can have a marking that reads "1st copy in a limited edition of 10" or "1 of 10" or "01/10" and so on. It's up to you how you want to identify your work. These details make books exclusive and collectible.

Packaging

Packaging protects the cartonero books from damage during shipping. Even if the envelope or packaging that you provide for your books suffers small amounts of damage during transportation, the book needs to be intact and in excellent condition when it arrives in the hands of readers. The majority of our books make long journeys, crossing Brazil and sometimes ending up in other countries, which is why it's crucial that they be packed properly.

Materials

To package our cartoneras, we use white glue, scissors, packing tape, kraft paper, plastic packaging, bubble wrap, and envelopes. The bubble wrap pads the books and protects them while they're en route, keeping their edges safe during the shipping and handling that all mail goes through.

Small packages. For small packages, the books are placed in plastic packaging to protect them from moisture. Later, they're wrapped in bubble wrap, which is fastened with packing tape to protect it from impact. Then we place the wrapped books inside envelopes. We use glue to seal the top flap of the envelope and wide packing tape to reinforce all the side flaps to protect against tearing.

<u>Larger packages</u>

For larger packages, we also make a reinforced bundle out of kraft paper. Because shipping to most places can take days or weeks, it's important that the books be protected enough to withstand the wear and tear of being shipped long distances.

We want our books to arrive completely intact to our readers, which is why we spend extra time to specially wrap them.

Shipping

We ship our cartonera books through the Brazilian post office, which is currently the only one we have access to, because accessing the services of a logistics and parcel shipping company requires a lot of financial resources. You need a lot of patience to use the post office, because the customer service varies a lot from one branch to another. Ask for information at the branch you plan on using, and always stay up to date on the company's website or through the news regarding the constantly changing rules for sending media mail.

Sales

There are countless possibilities for selling cartonero books and you're probably already thinking about one of them right now. Cartonera books can be sold in person, on social media, in physical and online stores, via newsletters, at artisanal markets, and from collectively run stores.

We started selling our books via announcements made on our blog *Bibliotecas do Brasil* and on social media sites like Twitter and Facebook. Payment was collected via bank deposit using e-payment services. In October of 2016, we launched our online store (loja.bibliotecasdobrasil.com). There are numerous web-store services available on the internet. To build a store, we read a lot and watched hours of videos to understand how they work. There's a very stimulating world on YouTube of people sharing their experiences and valuable information on how to handle financial issues, webstores, personal development, and marketing. If you want to set up a webstore, you're going to need to develop administrative skills. For those in Brazil, Sebrae offers online content for anyone who wants to set up an online store.

Maintaining a webstore requires responsibility, commitment, and honesty, because you're dealing with the financial resources of people who are interested in your work. Making cartonero books and selling them online is work, it's a paid occupation, and it demands a lot of you, because you're putting your name on the line. Producing handcrafted books and maintaining an online store is a process of constant learning, and people who partake in the activity never stop encountering, understanding, and handling issues that crop up along the way. It's something you do for yourself and for the people interested in your publications. It's a mutual exchange that benefits both parties.

Publicity

Your work won't advertise itself, at least not at first. Until the news starts spreading on its own, you need to work hard on advertising. As artists and writers, we need to learn how to share our work and create our own visibility. Share your work. It's part and parcel of the work all independent artists do to find people interested in learning about, appreciating, and buying their creations. At Magnolia Cartonera, we've created art entirely dedicated to advertising the release of books on our blogs, on social media, and in our newsletter. That way, we stoke the interest and curiosity of our readers in buying our books.

Part 4
Creation

A visual identity harmonizes all the book's elements, making communication more effective between the person who wrote the book and the person who is going to read it.

The cover can define the book's personality, but what's inside is crucial to reading and ingesting the content. The visual identity is a supplement to attract people's eyes and stoke their interest, not to mention it makes the reading experience more enjoyable.

If you write with a computer or laptop, you probably already have basic knowledge of how to use text editors like Microsoft Word. But if you write in a notebook or notepad and want to start publishing cartonero books, take this as an opportunity to learn how to use digital tools in your writing or artistic pursuits.

Publishing a book is important work and you'll need to develop some skills, like laying out a text document. These are some tips for the visual identity of your book, but they are all optional. Use them according to your personal preference, ability to complete them, and with the resources you have available.

Writing the Book

We write our books in Google Docs, a free text editing service. The program is easy to use and acts as a backup for any changes we make to the text, and it can be shared with as many people as you want.

When we write our books, we share the text with each other so we can both can edit, suggest ideas, trade information, and get it ready to be turned into a book. The fact that the program is online and can be used on any computer with access to the internet gives us greater freedom to access the book's file from multiple computers, whether we're at home, in a library, at places with free wi-fi like cafes and bookstores, or on our smartphones.

These are some of the programs we use to develop the visual aspect and between parentheses are free alternatives: Photoshop (Gimp), InDesign (Scribus), and Illustrator (Inkscape). If you want to dive deep into these specific programs, you can find online tutorials, free courses, and talk to people you know who know how to use them. These are just examples of what we do in our own cartonera practice. Choose what's best for you to get the job done.

Elements of a Visual Identity

Names

Within the first few pages, make sure to share information about your book to help readers identify where it came from. Put the name of the author and the people who created the illustrations, art, and/or photographs included in the book. Name the people responsible for the editing and handcrafting. If you work in a collective, identify each person that worked on the project. Also, put the name of the cartonera publisher involved in the project or who published it. Name the city and state where the book was thought up. Specify the edition and year of publication and the number of each copy.

Credits

If you use the work of other artists, you need to name them. Provide links to the artists' websites and information about the art used in your book. Read more about credits in part 6 of this book on Credits and Support.

Contact

Share contact information so that people can communicate with you, like emails, social media accounts, addresses, or P.O. boxes. Create an email exclusively for your cartonera activities to make your work look more professional.

Logo

A logo is your work's signature, it's a symbol created to identify it. The logo represents your brand and serves as your identity as an artist or author. It can be an abstract or figurative drawing, a symbol, or a name. You decide.

Fonts

When publishing a cartonero book, awaken your senses and think about choosing fonts that are legible to a wide variety of readers. Not everyone can read very small or ornate letters. If you use different fonts for the body of the text then you do for the titles, choose ones that combine in a visually harmonious way that facilitates reading. In the original Portuguese-language book, we used the following fonts that can be found for free online:

Lora size 14 pt for regular text

LLDidsco size 14 to 36 pt. for the titles

Pagination

This is another visual element that can be added to the book. Placing consecutive numbers on the pages helps readers easily find the information they desire.

Index

This is a list with names of the main chapters or topics, along with the page numbers where they can be found. It facilitates reading and finding information within the text. An index is optional and can be used when the book addresses multiple topics or has lots of chapters.

Chapters

These are the principal points within the body of text, generally defined by a title, a number, or both. Chapters can be thematic, dedicated entirely to explaining concepts and ideas in non-fiction books, or can develop characters in novels.

Colored pages

You can find printer paper and other types of paper in different colors, in pastel tones, and in neon in stores that sell school supplies or that sell different types of paper. We use colored title pages in lots of our books and on the covers of the Magnolia Zine.

Color printing

Color printing your cartonero is also an option for those who wish to embrace it and can be done on a home printer or at copy stores and printing presses who offer the service. If you have the means to do color printing, take advantage. Color printing requires a larger budget to finance the ink and/or out-sourcing of the work.

One compromise is to make some of the inside details colored, so you only have to color print the pages with those details. Those details raise the price of production and can make printing a more complex aspect of the production side, but the beauty of cartonera publications is that the possibilities exist for those who wish to try them. If you work in screen printing and want to print that way, go right ahead.

Backup

Back up everything you write. The backup of your online writing is just as important as the backup of your physical notebook or notepad. It allows your data to be restored if you lose the originals, which can be caused by accidental deletion or data corruption on your computer. If you prefer to use Word to write and your computer suffers an accident, you need to have a copy of the file or the document accessible in another location. Having backups is important, because if your computer is irreversibly damaged, you'll have a way to get your writing back. We use Google Docs, where the documents are stored in the data storage "cloud."

If you tend to write in a notebook or notepad you carry in your purse or bag, you need to have a notebook that never leaves your house, office, or writing space. Anthropologists who do field research tend to carry a small notebook in their bags with a pen attached by some yarn. When they return from the field with the data collected in their notebooks, they transfer the information to a computer or to a main logbook that they never remove from their research center, office, or classroom to avoid accidents, loss, and theft. Take stock of what it would mean for you and your project to lose the digital file or notebook where all the information for your book is centralized.

Work wisely and guarantee at least one copy of everything you write. The same advice applies to image archives and layout templates when you develop the visual aspects of your book.

Part 5
Security Tips

Cutting and Punching Tools

We use cutting and punching tools when crafting our cartoneras like box cutters, awls, needles, and scissors. When you offer workshops or do book making with groups of people, it will be your responsibility to guarantee that they know the tools and use them as safely as possible to avoid accidents. Care when using tools is important so that people don't hurt themselves or those around them. Use these tips for your own personal practice as well.

Do workshops with people who are mature enough to use the tools and always supervise their work. Lessons should be flexible and adaptable to the physical needs of the participants. If you're working with elderly people or people with disabilities or mobility issues, understand the needs of each and adapt your workshop to those needs. In our workshops, some people have had an easier time cutting cardboard and punching holes in the pages while standing, while others have felt more comfortable doing those activities sitting down. Some people have wanted to paint the cardboard seated on the floor because it feels better to them. Some people are left-handed, and others are right-handed, and those traits make a huge difference when it comes to cutting, painting, and sewing books. It takes a lot of conscious effort not to impose one way of cutting the cardboard or using the tools, because each person has their own traits and needs. Be observant and take note of what is most comfortable for each of them, and develop your abilities to integrate those needs into whatever activities you're undertaking together.

During workshops, guarantee that they can identify the best position to complete activities and let them be free to decide to stand or sit. But always give guidance about safety.

Using the Tools

Do all activities carefully, and when working with scissors, cutters, and awls, always hold the tools by the handles. When using cutting and punching tools, pay attention to your movements so the tools don't slip in your hands. Avoid doing multiple tasks at once where you have to use sharp tools. Do one activity at a time. Never play around or perform fast movements with the scissors, box cutter, or awl in your hands. Inappropriate movements can cause injury to the person holding the tool or others nearby. Guarantee a distraction-free environment in your workshops, but always reinforce that people should be responsible when using tools.

Stay Calm

Being an artisan requires that you come from a place of inner calm, patience, and consistency. Be mindful of how you use your tools within your cartonera practice. You will handle needles, cutters, scissors, and punching tools, and rushing and/or being distracted creates accidents. Sudden injury may require immediate treatment, interrupting your work to deal with the pain or the tool, and may require you to reprint the book if it becomes stained.

This work requires calm and care with yourself and the other people participating. Take the process of crafting your cartoneras as a chance to slow down and appreciate your art. Create a profound and real connection with your work.

Box Cutters

The box cutter requires a lot of attention due to the sharp blade and the constant repetition of use. If used incorrectly, it can cut your hands, fingers, and arms. It is important to take precautions to help keep everyone safe when using box cutters.

Before starting any cartonera activity, explain to the people participating that the cutting and punching tools should never be pointed directly at another person, because it is very dangerous and also not cool. Each person should use the box cutter in their own personal work area and never pass it to someone else with the blade exposed. The blade should be completely retracted before the cutter is handed to another person.

The box cutter blades are retractable, and in some models, there is a locking mechanism that allows the blade to remain fixed in a chosen position. The person using the cutter can decide how much of the blade to leave exposed for the most comfortable and efficient use. For large, professional-use box cutters, 3cm of exposed blade is enough for easy use (two or three sections of the blade). By keeping the blade short, pressure is applied with more precision to the cardboard, reducing the chances of it breaking or slipping. Guarantee that the table or flat surface where you do your work is not wobbly, and that the cutting mat is fully supported. Make sure to unlock and retract the blade completely to avoid accidents and injury. To save yourself effort while cutting cardboard, replace the blade whenever you notice it has become dull or is difficult to cut with. Using too much force when cutting can make the blade slip. When disposing of blade tips, make sure to wrap each piece to avoid injuring sanitation workers.

Scissors

Scissors need to be handled with the same care as box cutters, since they have sharp blades. Use scissors and other tools on top of tables or whatever supportive surface you do your work on. Once you've used the scissors, close the blades completely and place them back on the table. When passing scissors to someone else, close the blades completely, grab them, and hand them to the other person so that they can take the scissors by the handles. Avoid dropping tools on the floor to prolong their durability. Make sure the people in your collective are using tools safely and wisely and know how to handle them.

Paint

Research brands and buy the ones you know or that have been recommended to you by someone you trust. Depending on your sensitivities, paint can cause adverse allergic reactions. Whenever you paint your cartonera books, find ventilated areas or paint near an open window.

If you're painting with a group or in a workshop, talk to people you think might have an allergic reaction to the paint. If someone has a sensitivity, consider using gloves for protection and a disposable mask, both of which can be found at packaging stores, pharmacies, and in stores that sell safety equipment. If you have physical reactions to the paint, if you get headaches, dizzy, severe mood swings, or feel bad, leave the project for a while and get some air. These symptoms can be a sign that you need to take precautions. If they persist or return, seek medical attention.

First Aid Kit

Regardless of how much care and attention you dedicate while making cartonera books, accidents happen and even the most experienced people can get hurt. You can put together a kit with a few important items to have on hand if needed. Here are some suggestions:

Hygiene

• antibacterial ointment or gel

• mild soap

• wet wipes

• saline solution

Bandages

• band-aids

• gauze

• cotton pads

• surgical tape

• cotton swabs

Part 6
Credits and Support

The Importance of Giving Artists Credit

When using other artists' work, you absolutely must give them credit, because it shows respect for their intellectual property rights. By giving credit to artists and writers, we show our admiration for their work and valorize their creative contributions to the world.

We need to educate ourselves correctly about the importance of always crediting creators in all fields, be they writers of books or blogs, photographers, visual artists, etc. We need to be the people most interested in circulating information about the work of authors we like, because that's a way we can contribute to the visibility of their art.

As the author Austin Kleon says in his book *Show Your Work* (2014) and on his blog, "It's the right thing to do."

Giving credit provides information about the person who did the work you're sharing. If it's a photo, it should contain the name of the person who took the photo and a link to their website or social media accounts. If it's an excerpt from a book, it needs to have the author's name and the name of the book where the excerpt came from. You can even put a link directly to an online bookstore or the person's webstore so that readers can buy the book there.

If you're looking for images online and find an incredible image you'd like to use, you can't say it doesn't have an owner just because it was on Google Image Search. With a few clicks, it's easy to discover who the photo belongs to or the website where it was published. Never use other people's photos to sell classes, workshops, products, or services without their knowledge and permission. If you use the work of any artist on social media, always use the information after the @ (@magnoliacartonera), which creates a link to their social media profile, the artist's website or fan page (www.magnoliacartonera.com), or the # (*#magnoliacartonera*).

By correctly crediting artists and writers, not only are we maintaining the integrity of their rights, we're also collaborating in sharing their work. By correctly giving credit, we help the artists we admire expand their audience and find potential readers, as well as people who understand the value of their art, buy their books, and offer paid work opportunities.

Supporting Cartonero Books

It's us, readers of conscience, who must work together so that the cartonero books that enchant us have better chances of ending up in the hands of more people, on bookshelves, and in libraries, thus maintaining the ongoing cycle of reading and mutual support.

Any spontaneous support we can give as readers to cartonera books is extremely important. By sharing information on social media, recommending books to friends, and talking about the work with our partners in life, in work, and in the struggle, we generate interest in and curiosity about cartonero books.

Recommending useful texts to more people is also an essential way of supporting authors working with cartoneros, artisans, and independent artists who aren't well known to the larger public.

We need to raise awareness about the importance of financially supporting artist's artistic and literary output. Paying for a cartonero book dignifies the work and artistic and literary production of artisanal authors and artists. When we as readers buy cartonero books, we make the production of the book we hold in our hands, not to mention future titles being written at this exact moment, financially viable.

To pay for a cartonero book is to recognize the work of the people who dedicate themselves to its composition through writing, illustrating, painting the covers, binding, as well as all the intellectual work necessary for that publication to become a reality.

By buying cartonero books we are acknowledging the ideas of their authors and embracing their influence on our reading practices and lives. And by financially compensating independent authors for their work, we're collaborating directly with them so they can forge new paths to better live through their art. Our greatest hope is to see more appreciation for this literary, artisanal, and independent work in practice.

By buying cartonero books and paying what they're worth, we're materially recognizing all the work that goes into the project, from the collection of the cardboard boxes to their final form as a book, printed, bound and ready to be read by all kinds of people. Be they books by individual artists or people working in a collective, paying for the book is a way to recognize the efforts of creative people fighting to make ends meet at the end of the month just like everyone else. Paying for a cartonero book provides reasonable compensation for the work of artists and writers. Showing support in the form of likes on social media is important, but let's be honest, it's financial contributions that make art possible.

We should always keep in mind the financial adversities and restrictions that artists and writers on the margins face, creators who live anonymously in poverty without help, yet who nevertheless want themselves and their creations to flourish in legitimate ways, and who are searching for viable paths to make it happen. As people who admire books and independent artists, it's crucial that we be ready to pay for the amazing texts and art that are being created outside of conventional literary spaces. This is a show of respect and support for work that is not only artistically valid but also a lifeline for the vibrant and passionate practice of cartonera publishing.

Here at Magnolia Cartonera, it is our deepest desire to see more people who flourish as writers, editors, artists, and as individuals resisting in difficult times leading independent cartonero publishing projects and generating their own income through their art and writing. May this book be an inspiration and a guiding light to whoever wishes to start the journey.

Links

Links for further information

- sobre.magnoliacartonera.com

  Check out this book's bonus page where we share links to resources to help expand on what you've already learned. You'll find video tutorials on how to make cartonero books.

Bibliotecas do Brasil Store (Libraries of Brazil online store)

- loja.bibliotecasdobrasil.com

Blog Bibliotecas do Brasil (Libraries of Brazil Blog)

• www.bibliotecasdobrasil.com

Magnolia Cartonera

• www.magnoliacartonera.com

YouTube Channel

• youtube.com/bibliotecasdobrasil

Magnolia Cartonera Publications

Magnolia Cartonera is made up of Daniele Carneiro and Juliano Rocha. We are a couple dedicated to art and writing, and we create books whose goal is to amplify the autonomy of people and communities through simple and transformative solutions that we've already tested in practice. We hope our books educate and inspire people to throw themselves into their creative efforts without fear or prejudice. All our publications are available to buy on our online store: *loja.bibliotecasdobrasil.com*

Bibliotecas Mudam o Mundo (Libraries Change the World)
Daniele Carneiro and Juliano Rocha

• 108 pages

Bibliotecas Mudam o Mundo is a book about the future of conscious libraries using innovative and human examples. We share real stories of how libraries can become active and transformative institutions and have positive impacts on their communities. Libraries and initiatives that understand themselves as democratic spaces that promote inclusion and encourage other libraries through example to join in. The chapters address themes like diversity in libraries, libraries as refuge in times of instability, welcoming libraries and the need for free and public programming for marginalized or vulnerable communities, libraries that promote human development, the Maker Movement in libraries, and the movement Libraries Against Hate.

Guia Prático para Bibliotecas Comunitárias (A Practical Guide for Community Libraries)
Daniele Carneiro and Juliano Rocha

- 100 pages

- 2 educational posters

  A guide with tips on how to organize and develop your community library, free library, independent space, or autonomous project to promote reading that is open and accessible to all groups of people. Practical content on how to build an independent community library through self-management and with the resources available to you.

Ideias para Bibliotecas Livres (Ideas for Free Libraries)
Daniele Carneiro and Juliano Rocha

- 88 pages

- 2 posters

  A guide to creating free, community libraries that contains action plans, ideas, and suggestions to promote the circulation of books and creation of literacy and library projects. Build your free library, mini library, *geloteca*, *geladeiroteca* (community library initiatives using old refrigerators to house the books), book lending shelf, and other actions and initiatives that help books circulate among readers. With a book in hand and the tools we give you, start working on your project to incentivize reading today.

Eles Chegaram!/No Terminal (They're Here!/In the Terminal)
Juliano Rocha

A cartonero book in two parts. The first part is the post-apocalyptic story *Eles chegaram! (They're Here!)*, which narrates a day in the life of a man of unknown origins and his metaphysical discussions with brutish, incomprehensible, and terrifying beings, the content of which will chart a new course for humanity. The story includes 12 full-page, black-and-white illustrations. The second part of the book is a comic strip that portrays moments in the lives of people who travel through the city every day on public transportation, reflecting how these people live in urban areas. Scenes of solitude and old age, indigence and indifference, violence and solidarity are witnessed from inside the city bus and on all the stops along the way.

Cartonera Bibliotecas do Brasil
(Libraries of Brazil Cartonera Book)
Daniele Carneiro and Juliano Rocha

Essays on literature, reading experiences, libraries and free books, art and artists, writers, cinema, music, animal rights, the future, vulnerable people, human rights, solidarity, and much more. *Cartonera Bibliotecas do Brasil* is the first book published by blog *Bibliotecas do Brasil* in a cartonero format. The book has 80 pages of texts selected from the Newsletter Expresso (by the blog *Bibliotecas do Brasil* and Magnolia Cartonera) and an unreleased text by Daniele Carneiro and Juliano Rocha.

Free Content

Blog Bibliotecas do Brasil

A free, publicly accessible website for anyone providing key ideas on generating change in libraries and reading spaces. We share creative ideas, resources, and reports on initiatives, projects, and actions that incentivize autonomous reading that go unreported by mainstream media. *www.bibliotecas-dobrasil.com*

Newsletter Expresso

Periodic informational email with news, Magnolia Cartonera releases, and awesome, interesting, and fun information we select for readers with an optimistic, pleasant, and global outlook. Sign up for free at this link: *eepurl.com/dcRiTn*

YouTube Videos/Bibliotecas do Brasil

On our YouTube channel we share technical information and video tutorials on how we make the handcrafted books at Magnolia Cartonera. Use the videos alongside the knowledge you've learned from this book. *youtube.com/bibliotecasdobrasil*

Contact

If you liked this book and want to learn everything you can with us or gain a deeper understanding of our work, hire us for your literary event.

We talk about free and, community libraries, actions, and projects that incentivize literature, and independent publications like zines and cartonero books. We're available to consider proposals for paid talks, lectures, workshops, and cartonera displays in libraries, museums, schools, universities, cultural centers, fairs, and book festivals.

Send your proposal to contato@bibliotecasdobrasil.com.

Support our work

Your financial support helps our art prosper. Buy Magnolia Cartonera's books and zines at our online store so we can keep writing and publishing in-depth books on unpublished themes. We thank you for the support and your company.

July 2020